CHE GUEVARA
and the
IMPERIALIST REALITY

Mary-Alice Waters

PATHFINDER
NEW YORK LONDON MONTREAL SYDNEY

Copyright © 1998 by Pathfinder Press
All rights reserved

ISBN 978-0-87348-899-0
Library of Congress Control Number 2009929622

Manufactured in Canada

First edition, 1998
Eighth printing, 2025

This article first appeared in the October 13, 1997, issue of the *Militant*, a socialist newsweekly published in New York.

COVER PAINTING: Patrick Heron, *Five Disks:* 1963, oil on canvas, 167.6 x 152.4 cm © 1998 Artists Rights Society (ARS), New York / DACS, London

COVER: Toni Gorton

PATHFINDER
pathfinderpress.com
Email: pathfinder@pathfinderpress.com

Introductory note

THE FOLLOWING ARTICLE was circulated to participants in the conference on "The Twenty-First Century: The Legacy and Relevancy of Che's Works," held in Havana, Cuba, September 25–27, 1997, and was the basis of a presentation to that gathering by Mary-Alice Waters. The conference, sponsored by *Tricontinental* magazine and the Organization of Solidarity of the Peoples of Africa, Asia, and Latin America (OSPAAAL), was one of the activities commemorating the thirtieth anniversary of the revolutionary campaign waged in Bolivia by Ernesto Che Guevara and his comrades.

Guevara was one of the central leaders of the Cuban revolution, which brought down the U.S.-backed Batista dictatorship in 1959 and, in response to mounting pressure from Washington, opened the socialist revolution in the Americas. In 1966–67, he led a nucleus of revolutionaries from Bolivia, Cuba, and Peru fighting to overthrow the military dictatorship in Bolivia. In the process they sought to forge a Latin America–wide movement of workers and peasants that could lead the battle for land reform and against U.S. imperialist domination of the continent and advance the struggle for socialism. Guevara was wounded and captured on October 8, 1967. He was shot the next day by the Bolivian military, after consultation with Washington.

"Che Guevara and the Imperialist Reality" appeared in issue no. 138 of *Tricontinental,* OSPAAAL's magazine, published in Havana in English and Spanish editions.

Mary-Alice Waters is the editor of *New International* magazine and president of Pathfinder Press.

Che Guevara and the imperialist reality

BY MARY-ALICE WATERS

"TWENTY-ONE YEARS have elapsed since the end of the last world conflagration, and various publications in every language are celebrating this event, symbolized by the defeat of Japan. A climate of optimism is apparent in many sectors of the different camps into which the world is divided." Yet, "it is appropriate to ask whether this peace is real."[1]

These were the words with which Ernesto Che Guevara opened his 1966 Message to the Tricontinental, "Create two, three . . . many Vietnams: That is the watchword."

These words are an appropriate place to begin today—not only because this message, Che's last major political article, was published thirty years ago in the magazine that has taken the initiative to bring together the participants in this international symposium. Far more important is the fact that Che's Message to the Tricontinental so

---

1. Ernesto Che Guevara, "Vietnam and the World Struggle for Freedom," in *Che Guevara Speaks* (New York: Pathfinder, 1967, 2000), pp. 191–92 [2024 printing].

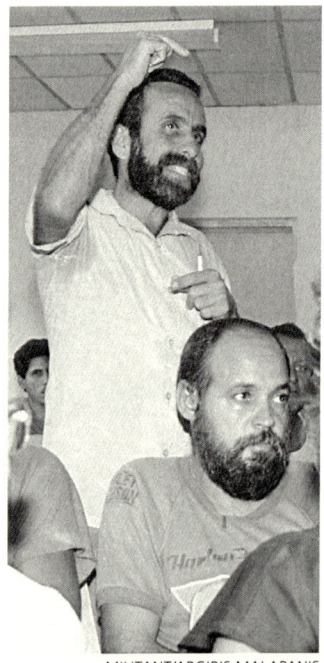
MILITANT/ARGIRIS MALAPANIS

MILITANT/MARGRETHE SIEM

PETER TURNLEY/©CORBIS

"We must keep in mind that imperialism is a world system, the final stage of capitalism, and that it must be beaten in a great worldwide confrontation." Clockwise from top left, worker in Cuban dairy factory participates in 1994 national debate on policies to confront economic crisis; UPS strikers rally in New Jersey in 1997; road from Kuwait City to Basra, Iraq, after U.S. invasion in February 1991.

accurately depicts the imperialist reality of the world we seek to change, the reality we must face unflinchingly if our anti-imperialist struggle is to be victorious, within the United States as elsewhere.

The relationship of class forces in a world still dominated by imperialism has shifted in favor of the oppressed and exploited.

Che's words remind us how well he understood the world in which, at the side of Fidel and others, he helped lead the working people of Cuba to establish the first free territory of the Americas and open a new chapter in the history of the modern working-class movement. They help focus our attention on the most important change that has occurred over the thirty years since Che's death: the fact that the relationship of class forces in a world still dominated by imperialism—with ups and downs, advances and setbacks—has shifted in favor of the oppressed and exploited.

The post–World War II economic and social order christened by Washington's heinous flood of fire against the people of Hiroshima and Nagasaki is still with us. But the "climate of optimism" Che pointed to in 1966 is no more. Today's climate is rather one of foreboding among the imperialist masters, marked by short periods of "irrational exuberance" (to quote the top central banker serving the U.S. rulers) and lengthening periods of gloom; heightened anxiety among the middle classes of all countries who count on the propertied rulers for protection and stability; social polarization marked by aggressive probes by rightist and incipient fascist currents; and, most important of all, signs of resistance and rising defensive struggles among those from whose labor capital extracts surplus value in an attempt to reverse its long-term crisis.

In the United States, for the first time in years, an important section of the working class nationwide, the UPS (United Parcel Service) workers organized by the Teamsters union, emerged victorious from a hard-fought strike that drew popular support in the United States as well as worldwide attention. A new preoccupation is palpable in serious bourgeois circles in the United States, as they face the prospect of more frequent and more successful working-class resistance to declining real wages, accelerated speedup, two-tier pay scales, and other stratagems that seek to divide workers and weaken solidarity on the job. The employers are also considering the upsetting implications for their precarious economic health of the possibility that defensive battles by workers may set an example and bring weighty reinforcements to other social struggles—against police brutality, for immigrants' rights, in support of women's equality, against racist discrimination.

The United States is no exception in this regard. Throughout the imperialist world, and especially in Europe, the pattern of growing resistance and sharpening class conflict is evident.

Those who dominated the other two "sectors of the different camps into which the world is divided"—to whom Che referred almost thirty years ago and who, as he noted, shared the "climate of optimism" with imperialism's ruling families—also find the weather sharply changed. The bureaucratic castes that dominated much of what was termed the socialist camp today find themselves in disarray as they run after a declining capitalist system. And the bourgeoisies of the third world—from Mexico to Malaysia—are discovering the awful truth that the so-called miracle of emerging market economies doesn't culminate in emerged industrially advanced capitalist countries, stable currencies, and broadening well-being, but leads instead to explosive instability and increased domination and ownership by all the parasitic forms of imperial capital. Both these formerly optimistic ruling elites today confront urban and rural toilers in greater numbers, toilers increasingly impatient with the long wait for the promised capitalist prosperity for all.

The peace was not real

The dawn of the twenty-first century brings with it not a new international order but speculative frenzies and growing capitalist division and disarray. Che was right: the peace was not real. And it has not been real—no matter how often proclaimed—since the nuclear annihilation of Hiroshima and Nagasaki registered the ascendancy, and the true face, of the North American colossus. As the socialist newsweekly, the *Militant,* said in its banner headline the week of Tokyo's surrender to Washington in August 1945: "There is no peace!"

That has been the truth not only of the second half of the twentieth century but remains so for the opening of the twenty-first. It has marked the course of the imperialist powers toward the peoples of the semicolonial world and the workers states ever since the Yankee ascendancy—and more and more indicates the future of relations among the capitalist powers themselves, as well. The convulsions we are living through are products of the increasing exhaustion of the world order that emerged from the flames and ashes of World War II with U.S. imperialism then near the pinnacle of its power.

Fifty years ago Washington's imperialist rivals/allies were desperate for loans and industrial goods to rebuild. The toiling peoples of the Soviet Union who heroically carried the brunt of resistance to German imperialism's invading forces—war weary, and facing colossal reconstruction tasks—seemed more vulnerable than ever before. But U.S. imperialism's great hopes began to evaporate even before they could be born, as the conscript ranks of the U.S. armed forces, workers and farmers in uniform, refused to allow themselves to be used against the rising tide of the colonial revolution. In mass demonstrations of a size and sweep unprecedented in the history of modern warfare, U.S. soldiers, sailors, and members of the merchant marine—from France to the Pacific bases—said, "No, we're going home!"[2] Through the breach, over the next decade, the fighting toilers of the colonial world sacrificed mightily but advanced—from China, to India, Indonesia, Vietnam, Korea, Egypt, and further—driving out their weakened former colonial masters.

The banner of national liberation and independence, unfurled worldwide during the war and postwar years, continued its triumphal advance up to and through the victory of the Cuban workers and farmers in 1959 and then their deepening socialist revolution that distanced them from the capitalist orbit and enabled them to face down the Yankee colossus.

The "climate of optimism" Che noted in 1966 was the product of a quarter century of accelerated economic expansion, with rates of growth whose memory make the

---

2. See "1945: When U.S. Troops Said 'No!'" by Mary-Alice Waters, in *New International* no. 7 (1991).

capitalists weep today. This expansion was fueled, first, by massive war production and productivity increases, and then by the extensive renewal of capital made necessary and possible by the historically unprecedented scope of the wartime destruction of plant and equipment in Europe, Japan, and much of Asia, as well as by the prior horrendous defeats of the working-class movement in many of these countries. But the growth of profit rates and increasing rate of expanded production that undergirded the postwar capitalist dream and imperialist power were already beginning to wane even as Che wrote.

The reality is a growing gap between prosperity and well-being for a few and increasing insecurity, misery, and impoverishment of the great majority.

Today, after a quarter century of declining profit rates—despite brutal "cost-cutting" drives against the wages and living standards of working people in all sectors of the world—the world capitalist economy is in the midst of a long-term deflationary crisis, marked by growing instability, financial volatility, and mercurial giddiness underlying bourgeois opinion. Trade and currency conflicts are intensifying. Balloons of capitalist debt, created by forcing larger and larger loans on semicolonial governments and businesses, expand and then deflate with increasing speed. From the collapse of the Mexican peso a few years ago, to the currency crisis shaking the Asian "tigers" today, to the looming prospect of devaluation in Hong Kong or Brazil tomorrow, to the highest levels of unemployment in Germany since the coming to power of the Nazi regime—such events are only slightly hidden forms of the dollar crisis and the growing instability and weakness of the imperialist powers, including the Yankee colossus. They are harbingers of more, much more, to come.

Beneath the braggadocio about the global "market miracle"—and its "theoretical" rationalizations that go by names such as the "New Era" and the "New Paradigm"—lies the reality of a growing gap between prosperity and well-being for relatively narrow layers of the better-off middle classes, on the one hand, and, on the other, increasing insecurity, misery, and impoverishment of the great majority. This is the actuality from the city streets and rural villages of Mexico, Peru, Argentina, and Haiti, to those in Egypt, India, Thailand, and Indonesia; from the refugee camps of war-torn Africa, to the mines, factories, and farms of Russia; from the working-class suburbs of major European cities, to the swelling ranks of working families newly denied food stamps and medical aid in the U.S. land of milk and honey.

At the opening of this decade, the U.S. rulers briefly trumpeted the dawn of a "new world order," even "the end of history," in the wake of the White House–orchestrated and UN-camouflaged assault on Iraq—a murderous war on a sovereign nation exposed and denounced in the United Nations Security Council only by Cuba's representative, speaking with Che's spirit.[3] But Washington's promises of spreading peace, prosperity, and democracy throughout the

---

3. Fidel Castro and Ricardo Alarcón, *U.S. Hands Off the Mideast! Cuba Speaks Out at the United Nations* (New York: Pathfinder, 1990), edited with an introduction by Mary-Alice Waters.

region were merely cynical rationalizations for the use of military might to shore up a weakening imperial world order.

Today large parts of Yugoslavia are confronting not only the devastating consequences of the first land war in Europe in fifty years, but what is becoming a prolonged imperialist occupation. As Washington and its European rivals maneuver for position there, they are sinking their roots more and more deeply into the Balkans powder keg. The Clinton administration acknowledged two days ago what many both in Yugoslavia and the world over have long known—that neither Washington nor the other imperialist powers in NATO have any intention of withdrawing their troops from Bosnia next year or by any foreseeable date.

The U.S. rulers are pressing the expansion of NATO in Eastern Europe in order to reposition their troops closer to the heartland of the October Revolution and lay the basis to eventually accomplish by force what, to their dismay, they have failed to achieve in Russia and elsewhere in the former Soviet Union—restoration of the dominance of stable capitalist social relations.

Washington is rekindling the imperialist powers' "Great Game," as it pushes for domination of the vast Caspian oil reserves throughout the Caucasus and Central Asian republics of the former USSR. The basis for renewed assaults against Iran grows apace. The steady social and economic disintegration of sub-Saharan Africa is accompanied by increasingly frequent imperialist military interventions. The permanent garrisoning of tens of thousands of nuclear-armed U.S. troops on the Korean peninsula threatens another holocaust on an even greater scale than that inflicted on workers and peasants there almost half a century ago. And on the opposite end of this island where we are meeting today, the U.S.

government still maintains a military base at Guantánamo on illegally occupied Cuban soil, a dagger always ready for whatever provocation Washington deems useful. U.S. president William Clinton can arrogantly assert, as he did in his second inaugural address last January, that "America stands alone as the world's indispensable nation." And the new secretary of state chosen by Clinton to personify the direction of his second term can and will pursue the aggressive and insolent foreign policy born of such historical miscalculation. But we are far from a unipolar world in which a declining Yankee empire reigns supreme as "the indispensable nation." Between the opening salvos of World War III, already sounded from Iraq to Bosnia, and those of a new global conflagration stand countless defensive battles that will be waged by the toiling classes who constitute the "indispensable answer" for humanity. They will have their chance to take their own destiny in hand and determine the course of history.

The world of capitalist disorder—the imperialist reality of the twenty-first century—would not be strange to Che. Nor would he fail to recognize the weight, power, and political leverage of the Cuban revolution within this reality. Far from being dismayed by the odds we face, moreover, he would have examined this world with scientific precision and charted a course to win, turning toward the battles with the warrior's spirit he was imbued with.

The imperialist enemy is weaker
Four points call out for emphasis in relationship to Che and the imperialist reality:
   1. Che's scientific understanding of the world in which we live and fight drew deeply on the continuity of the modern

working-class movement, on the cumulative lessons of the battles we have won, and the battles we have lost over the last 150 years—from the foundations laid by Marx and Engels, through the continuity forged by Lenin and the Bolshevik revolution whose eightieth anniversary we celebrate a few weeks from now. Che understood, profoundly, the character of the enemy we face: that imperialism is a world system—the last stage of capitalism, a system ruled by the law of value—and that the world class struggle is an interrelated whole. Proletarian internationalism is not a luxury, or one among several effective choices; it is dictated by capital itself, by its inevitable national conflicts and its rapacious character. Che knew that proletarian internationalism is a precondition for the working class to surmount the competition among ourselves inherent in the condition of propertyless wage slavery, to rise to a level of discipline and culture necessary to win, and to transform ourselves in the process.

"Let it be known that we have measured the scope of our acts and that we consider ourselves no more than a part of the great army of the proletariat," Che wrote in his Message to the Tricontinental.[4]

"We must definitely keep in mind that imperialism is a world system, the final stage of capitalism," Che said in that article, "and that it must be beaten in a great worldwide confrontation. The strategic objective of that struggle must be the destruction of imperialism. . . . In focusing on the destruction of imperialism, it is necessary to identify its head, which is none other than the United States of North America."[5]

---

4. *Che Guevara Speaks,* p. 208.

5. *Che Guevara Speaks,* p. 203.

Over and over, taking advantage of the broadest public forums, including some arenas not used to hearing the truth fearlessly spoken—at the 1961 Organization of American States–sponsored conference in Punta del Este, Uruguay; at the 1964 United Nations Conference on Trade and Development in Geneva; before the UN General Assembly later that same year; at the 1965 Afro-Asian solidarity conference in Algiers—Che dissected and exposed the political and economic workings of the imperialist system. And he did so with profound understanding, unflinching truthfulness, and a trenchant humor that instilled confidence in working people and revolutionary fighters the world over.

Che dissected and exposed the political and economic workings of the imperialist system.

In Cuba, as he fulfilled his many leadership responsibilities, Che labored—day in and day out—to strip bourgeois obfuscation from questions of political economy and to assure workers access to knowledge of the economics and politics of socialism, so they could increasingly and confidently assert control over the organization and administration of labor and all aspects of production.

He sought to instill in the Cuban workers and farmers a consciousness of the stakes involved and of their historic role on the front lines of confrontation with the "great enemy of the human race," as he accurately labeled U.S. imperialism in his Message to the Tricontinental. No accommodation is possible, he taught us, and, more importantly, no loss of nerve ever occurs without a consequent strengthening of the class enemy.

"Those who know recent history know that you can't play with imperialism," Che told the assembled workers at the INPUD, the National Industry of Domestic Utensils and Products in July 1964. "[Brazilian president] Goulart is out, exiled in Uruguay, just to show how you can't play with imperialism. And [Dominican dictator] Trujillo is no more, demonstrating even better that you can't play with imperialism; because when Trujillo put his personal interests above the interests of the empire and decided to make his own policy—after having amassed a huge fortune with the help of the same North Americans, from the blood and sweat of his people—when it came to that moment of rebellion, he was simply liquidated.

"And the same thing happened to the Vietnam puppet [Ngo Dinh Diem] who thought for a moment that he could blackmail the North Americans. This is a dangerous game. The North Americans cannot be blackmailed; they go directly after what they want and they know what they want. In order to face up to the North Americans, it is necessary to speak in a very clear and straight way and to put aside any thought of placing life ahead of principle, just as our people have done on repeated occasions; and beyond the government there must be a whole people armed and prepared to defend it."[6] The lesson for fighting workers and farmers and uncompromising rebel youth in the world today could not be more succinctly put.

One of the most perceptive—if unintentional—tributes to Che in this thirtieth anniversary year appeared a few

---

6. Guevara, in *Escritos y discursos* (Havana: Editorial Ciencias Sociales, 1985), vol. 8, p. 143.

weeks ago in the letters column of one of the main organs of the United Kingdom's ruling class, *The Times* of London. Almost as if trying to illustrate Che's words just quoted, the author of the letter, Maurice Baird-Smith—writing from retirement in southern France, in the inimitable style of the moneyed British—recalled the following:

> Sir, The return of the remains of Che Guevara to Cuba (The World in Brief, July 14) brings back vivid memories of the contacts I had with him in the early 1960s when I was director of an international oil company in Havana which was sequestered by the Cuban Government.
>
> "El Che" was an out and out Communist who never hid his belief that we should be got rid of. To visit him in his office was an unforgettable experience. He sat in "battle dress" with two pistols on the desk pointing at me. He was always very courteous but left no doubt that he was dealing with an organisation which he felt the world could well do without.

Quite.

The representatives of imperialism, confronted by the power of the Cuban working class as it took its own destiny in hand, have never forgotten, nor will they ever forgive, the lessons they were taught.

2. Guevara was one of the few leaders of world stature who understood and explained with unvarnished clarity that the successful resistance to U.S. imperialist aggression being mounted by the Vietnamese people represented a turning point in the history of the twentieth century that would

have far-reaching consequences worldwide. In issuing his call to "create two, three . . . many Vietnams," Che accurately noted that the ability of the Vietnamese to hold off the weighty military machine of U.S. imperialism was unprecedented—despite being "tragically alone," from the standpoint of economic and military aid commensurate with their needs.

The successful resistance to U.S. imperialism by the Vietnamese people represented a turning point in the history of the twentieth century.

"Defensive weapons, and not in sufficient number, are all these marvelous Vietnamese soldiers have besides love for their country, for their society, and a courage that stands up to all tests," Guevara stated in 1966. "But imperialism is bogged down in Vietnam. It sees no way out and is searching desperately for one that will permit it to emerge with dignity from the dangerous situation in which it finds itself."

At the same time, Che emphasized, "when we analyze the isolation of the Vietnamese we are overcome by anguish at this illogical moment in the history of humanity. U.S. imperialism is guilty of aggression. Its crimes are immense, extending over the whole world. We know this, gentlemen! But also guilty are those who at the decisive moment hesitated to make Vietnam an inviolable part of socialist territory—yes, at the risk of a war of global scale, but also compelling the U.S. imperialists to make a decision."[7]

---

7. *Che Guevara Speaks*, p. 195.

Most importantly, Che understood that the courage, dignity, and tenacity of the Vietnamese people in fighting for their sovereignty, for their freedom from subordination to the inhuman consequences of the laws of capital, had changed forever the political consciousness of millions living in the United States and was hastening the day of reckoning for U.S. imperialism.

The fact that U.S. soldiers confront "the permanent hostility of the entire population" in Vietnam, Guevara noted, is "provoking repercussions inside the United States. It is leading to the appearance of a factor that was attenuated by imperialism at full strength: the class struggle inside its own territory."[8]

It will be a long time, Che wrote, "before we know if President Johnson ever seriously intended to initiate some of the reforms needed by his people—to sandpaper the class contradictions that are appearing with explosive force and mounting frequency. What is certain is that the improvements announced under the pompous title of the Great Society have gone down the drain in Vietnam. The greatest of the imperialist powers is feeling in its own bowels the bleeding inflicted by a poor, backward country; its fabulous economy is strained by the war effort. Killing has ceased to be the most comfortable business for the monopolies."[9]

When those words were written, the escalation of Washington's aggression against Vietnam was scarcely two years old. Che did not live to see the extent of the explosion of

---

8. *Che Guevara Speaks*, p. 208.
9. *Che Guevara Speaks*, p. 195.

struggle inside the United States that finally linked up with the resistance of the Vietnamese people, defeating the mightiest military power on earth and altering the course of the last quarter century. But we should note that as a result of that historic struggle by the Vietnamese people, Washington's preoccupation with that war gave the hard-pressed people of Cuba time to breathe, and to redeem the courage of their fellow combatants in Indochina by consolidating a socialist revolution right on the doorstep of U.S. imperialism.

Che also correctly gauged the significance of the first mass actions inside the United States against the Vietnam war and the interconnection of this growing movement with the rising Black struggle. Che saw the unavoidable economic consequences of the war, from which neither Washington nor world finance capital would ever totally recover, and the beginning transformation of the working class within the borders of the United States—a transformation still not reversed, and one that cannot be short of titanic battles whose outcome no one can today guarantee.

3. Time and again Che returned to the vanguard role of the Black struggle in the U.S. working-class movement, underscoring the courage and combativity of the masses of African-American people whose struggles were then culminating in the destruction of the Jim Crow system of segregation that still prevailed in law throughout the southern states of the United States, and in fact in much of the rest of the country as well. He had an accurate appreciation of the social weight of the Black struggle and the substantial majority proletarian composition of the Black population. His judgment was consistent with the political vanguard role the Black freedom struggle has

played, from the days of Radical Reconstruction following the defeat of the slavocracy in the Civil War to the present resistance to the consequences of finance capital's domination.

By the mid-1960s, the mass proletarian battles against Jim Crow were just reaching their successful culmination—thanks in part to the powerful example and challenge posed by the Cuban revolution, it should be said. Upon taking power in January 1959, Cuba's revolutionary government began to enforce a sweeping ban on any forms of racial discrimination—just ninety miles from the shores of the old Confederacy. Pointing to the oppressed status of Blacks in the United States, as well as of immigrants from Latin America and Asia, Che effectively unmasked Washington's pretensions to teach the world about freedom and democracy.

"The United States intervenes in Latin America invoking the defense of free institutions," Che said in addressing the UN General Assembly in December 1964. "The time will come when this assembly will acquire greater maturity and demand of the United States government guarantees for the life of the Blacks and Latin Americans who live in that country, most of them U.S. citizens by origin or adoption.

"Those who kill their own children and discriminate daily against them because of the color of their skin; those who let the murderers of Blacks remain free, protecting them, and furthermore punishing the Black population because they demand their legitimate rights as free men—how can those who do this consider themselves guardians of freedom? . . . The government of the United States is not the champion of freedom, but rather the perpetuator of exploitation and oppression against the peoples of the world and against a large part of its own population."[10]

Che Guevara and Malcolm X

Che was a contemporary of Malcolm X, one of the greatest modern working-class leaders in the United States, and the two of them were drawn toward each other as kindred revolutionary fighters. Like Malcolm, Che was no disciple of any variant of the Gandhian strategy of nonviolence; they were bound by their shared courage, audacity, and commitment to win freedom "by any means necessary." Che and Malcolm were bound by their utter contempt for the prerogatives of capital and the pretensions of its personifiers; by their respect for and openness to the integrity and intelligence of every human being who stood up and fought; and by their common refusal to compromise the truth. They were bound by their unshakable confidence in the capacity of ordinary men and women to transform themselves in the process of fighting to transform the conditions of their existence and change the world. And by their disdain for the rationalizations and cowardice of the misleaders of the toilers.

During Guevara's 1964 visit to New York to address the United Nations General Assembly, he spent an evening talking with a group of journalists and writers who were supporters of the Cuban revolution. Excerpts from the discus-

---

10. "Cuba's Example Shows that the People of the World can Liberate Themselves," December 11, 1964, in Fidel Castro and Che Guevara, *To Speak the Truth: Why Washington's 'Cold War' against Cuba Doesn't End* (New York: Pathfinder, 1992), p. 155 [2024 printing]. Che's reply at the conclusion of the General Assembly debate later the same day also appears in this book.

sion were later broadcast on New York radio station WBAI. The 1964 Mississippi Freedom Summer had just drawn to a close, a summer of intense civil rights battles in the South during which, among other events, three young volunteers had been brutally murdered by Mississippi small businessmen and police officers in the Ku Klux Klan. Che was asked, "Considering the events of last summer . . . the recent events in Mississippi, how do you see the struggle of the Negro people in America?" His answer was careful but clear:

Che and Malcolm were bound by their unshakable confidence in the capacity of ordinary men and women to transform themselves in the process of fighting to transform the world.

"That's a very difficult question for me to answer," he said. "One would have to know all the reactions of the North American people as a whole, the relations among whites and Blacks, the capacity for response among the Black people, the capacity of the leaders. In short, we would have to know in great detail a lot of aspects that I do not know. In general, it seems that racial violence is flourishing in some North American states. In the face of that there are some means and ways. We can crouch a little more to see if the blow hurts less. We can energetically protest and then receive more blows. Or we can answer blow for blow. But that's very easy to say, and it's very difficult to do. And there must be preparation in order to do that. I don't know what the reaction would be, and what the possibilities of a reaction would be. I cannot predict it."[11]

During that same visit Malcolm invited Che to address a rally organized by the Organization of Afro-American Unity (OAAU) at the Audubon Ballroom in New York City. At the last minute, intelligence reports indicated that it would not be wise for Che to appear. The freedom of operations enjoyed by various counterrevolutionary Cuban outfits at that time had been demonstrated two days earlier when one of them, using a U.S. Army–issue rocket launcher, fired a bazooka shell at the United Nations building while Guevara was addressing the General Assembly. The shell fell short and landed harmlessly in the East River, but the explosion could be heard in the assembly hall. Che continued his speech without pause or notice.

Regretting that it was not possible for him to attend the OAAU meeting, Che sent greetings that were read to the appreciative audience by Malcolm. "I love a revolutionary," Malcolm said in introducing the message from Che. "And one of the most revolutionary men in this country right now was going to come out here along with our friend Sheik Babu [the leader of the Zanzibar liberation struggle and pioneer of Tanzanian independence], but he thought better of it. But he did send this message. It says:

"'Dear brothers and sisters of Harlem, I would have liked to have been with you and Brother Babu, but the actual conditions are not good for this meeting. Receive the warm salutations of the Cuban people and especially those of Fidel, who remembers enthusiastically his visit to Harlem a few years ago. United we will win.'"

---

11. Guevara, December 16, 1964, from unpublished transcript.

MILITANT/MARK SATINOFF

"Courage, dignity, and tenacity" of Vietnamese people sharpened class struggle in United States, hastening day of reckoning for U.S. imperialism. Above, New York protest against the war in Vietnam, 1972. Below, police attack opponents of Jim Crow segregation in U.S. south during 1963 Battle of Birmingham. Che Guevara pointed to the vanguard role of the Black struggle in the U.S. working-class movement.

Then Malcolm added: "I'm happy to hear your warm round of applause in return, because it lets the Man know that he's just not in a position today to tell us who we should applaud for and who we shouldn't applaud for. And you don't see any anti-Castro Cubans around here—we eat them up."[12]

Malcolm had a similar sense of appreciation of what the Chinese revolution had done to shatter racist lies and assumptions about oppressed peoples of color that had been perpetuated for centuries by the major colonial and then imperialist ruling classes of Europe and North America. Shortly before the rally at which Che had been scheduled to speak, Malcolm reminded another OAAU meeting in Harlem:

"There was a time in this country when they used to use the expression about Chinese, 'He doesn't have a Chinaman's chance.' Remember when they used to say that about the Chinese? You don't hear them saying that nowadays. Because the Chinaman has more chance now than they do. . . . It was not until China became independent and strong that the Chinese people all over the world became respected. . . . It's the same way with you and me."[13]

Is it any mystery why Che and Malcolm recognized and respected each other? Is it any wonder they were both hated and feared by the powerful forces whom they were determined to mobilize the oppressed and exploited to destroy?

---

12. Malcolm X, "At the Audubon," December 13, 1964, in *Malcolm X Speaks* (New York: Pathfinder, 1965), p. 136 [2022 printing].

13. Malcolm X, "The Homecoming Rally of the OAAU," November 29, 1964, in *By Any Means Necessary* (Pathfinder, 1970), p. 180 [2025 printing].

At a time when there were few among those who called themselves socialist or communist—in the United States or anywhere else in the world—who understood Malcolm's revolutionary trajectory and worked with him to advance it, Fidel and Che both were honored and proud to stand with him.

And I can add, with equal pride, that in the English-speaking world the predecessor of Pathfinder Press was the publishing house most closely associated at that time with the publication of the speeches and writings of both Malcolm X and of Che and Fidel.

4. Che was acutely conscious of the place of the Cuban revolution in world politics. He understood and lived the present as history. He knew Cuba's example was an objective factor not only in the nations oppressed by imperialism, but that the reach of this example extended into the imperialist countries themselves.

"What does the Cuban revolution teach? That revolution is possible." Those ringing words from the Second Declaration of Havana remain as true today as they were in 1962. The lesson remains the same.[14]

"I free Cuba from any responsibility, except that which stems from its example," Che wrote in his 1965 letter of farewell to Fidel.[15] And he knew better than any the power of that example. The revolutionary course and political character of Ernesto Che Guevara are inseparable from the Cuban revolution, and from the communist leadership he was part of and helped to forge. Che could not have be-

---

14. *The First and Second Declarations of Havana* (New York: Pathfinder, 1962, 1994, 2007), p. 70 [2025 printing].

15. "Farewell letter to Fidel," in *Che Guevara Speaks*, p. 187.

come the Che we know separate from the Cuban revolution. So it is appropriate, I believe, to close by singling out five points that underscore the historic weight of that revolution in Che's lifetime and since.

Rejecting 'revolution is not yet possible,' and substituting '*Sí se puede*,' Cuba changed the course of history.

• "Had we been willing to follow the schemas, we would not be gathered here today," Fidel reminded the Cuban people on July 26, 1988. "We would not have had a socialist revolution in this hemisphere. . . . Theory had it that no revolution could be made here; that's . . . what the manuals used to say."

"We drew our own conclusions starting from the principles of socialism," Fidel noted.[16]

The continuity of the Cuban revolution goes back not only to Martí and the Independence Wars but also through the October Revolution, the Paris Commune, and the origins of the modern workers movement in the rise of industrial capitalism. The leadership of the Cuban revolution broke with the self-serving theories of the international movement that looked to Moscow for political leadership, theories that were only the rationalizations of a social caste that had long beforehand abandoned the course of proletarian internationalism. The revolutionary struggle against

---

16. Fidel Castro, *Cuba Will Never Adopt Capitalist Methods* (New York: Pathfinder, 1988), pp. 21, 22 [2021 printing].

the U.S.-backed Batista dictatorship was carried through to its culmination in a victory that opened the door to socialist revolution.

Rejecting "revolution is not yet possible," and substituting *"Sí se puede,"* Cuba changed the course of history. As the leadership of the July 26 Movement mobilized workers and farmers in the revolution's opening year to carry out a thoroughgoing land reform and other measures in their class interests, the U.S. rulers reacted by organizing counterrevolutionary forces to overthrow the new government. Far from being cowed by escalating Yankee-organized assaults, however, Cuban working people and their leadership responded by deepening the revolution's proletarian course. On April 16, 1961, Fidel Castro—at a mass rally to honor victims of an imperialist-instigated air attack—proclaimed the socialist character of the Cuban revolution. And over the next three days the Cuban people in arms and their Revolutionary Armed Forces moved into action to crush the CIA-organized mercenary invasion at Playa Girón.

The mobilization of the Cuban toilers by the millions to realize the historic feat of opening the socialist revolution in the Americas confirmed in practice that revolution is possible, reknitting communist continuity back to the Bolsheviks and the founders of the modern working-class movement. For their audacity, Fidel, Che, and their comrades—like Lenin and Marx before them—were denounced as Jacobin adventurers by the majority of those who spoke as the leadership of the international workers movement.

Communist theory, Cuban workers and farmers confirmed with their lives, is the generalization of the line of march of a class. Communist practice is the fearless and uncompromising pursuit of that line of march. Because of the Cuban revolution, the danger of mistaking variants of social democracy or Stalinism for communism, or confounding petty-bourgeois radicalism with proletarian discipline, had been diminished. The revolutionary road was more clearly marked. As Che put it in his discussion with U.S. supporters of the Cuban revolution: "The revolutionary makes the revolution. But the revolution makes the revolutionary." To put it in the words of the young Marx, "the educator must himself be educated."[17]

• The rectification process that advanced with growing momentum in Cuba between 1986 and the end of 1989 was not simply an adjustment in priorities or an attempt to confront problems of increasing corruption. It was a "revolution within the revolution," as Fidel described it in November 1987,[18] like a ship correcting course while it continues full sail ahead. This process—promoted by Fidel Castro and other leaders of the revolution as a return to the kind of policies Che pioneered and defended—represented another historic example being set by the Cuban revolution.

Rectification became a social movement

Rectification marked the beginning of a turn away from the political course with regard to economic policy that had predominated in Cuba since the early 1970s, a period during which Che's rich legacy of practical activity and

---

17. Karl Marx, "Theses on Feuerbach," in Karl Marx and Frederick Engels, *Collected Works* (Moscow: Progress Publishers), vol. 5, p. 7.

18. Fidel Castro, speech closing City of Havana provincial party meeting, November 29, 1987, in the *Militant,* January 29, 1988. Also found in *Granma Weekly Review,* December 13, 1987.

theoretical contributions to building socialism was pushed aside. "[I]deas diametrically opposed to Che's economic thought began to take over," as Fidel put it ten years ago in a speech commemorating the twentieth anniversary of Guevara's death.[19] The system of economic management and planning used in one variant or another throughout the Soviet Union and Eastern Europe had been adopted during that earlier period, finding fertile enough ground in Cuba to flourish.

Rectification was an advance made possible not only by the continuing strength of the communist leadership in Cuba but even more importantly by the 1979 revolutionary victories in Nicaragua and Grenada that ended the isolation of Cuba's workers and farmers government in the Americas. It was an advance that gained impetus from the internationalist mission in Angola and the 1988 victory at Cuito Cuanavale, with all that battle exemplified for the anti-imperialist struggle in sub-Saharan Africa.

At its height, rectification took on the character of a growing social movement led by Cuba's most conscious and disciplined working people. Just as the bureaucratic parties and regimes of Eastern Europe and the USSR were beginning to shatter in face of irresolvable economic, social, and political crises that had been fostered for decades, the Cuban revolution was gaining strength along a proletarian political course. This renewal, Fidel explained in his October 1987 tribute to Che, would have given him

---

19. Fidel Castro, speech marking twentieth anniversary of the death of Ernesto Che Guevara, October 8, 1987, in Che Guevara, Fidel Castro, *Socialism and Man in Cuba* (Pathfinder, 1968, 1989, 2009), p. 54 [2024 printing].

much joy and confidence, just as Guevara would have been "appalled" by what had preceded it. Because, Fidel noted, Che "knew that communism could never be attained by wandering down those worn capitalist paths and that to follow along those paths would mean eventually to forget all ideas of solidarity and even internationalism."[20]

- Without rectification having been initiated and led—gaining momentum in the mass working-class vanguard before the special period became a fact of life—the Cuban revolution could never have successfully confronted and prevailed in face of its most difficult years. At the opening of this decade, the abrupt decline in aid and trade on favorable terms with the disintegrating regimes of the Soviet bloc precipitated the most severe economic crisis since 1959, compounded by ongoing and unrelenting economic warfare long ago instigated and organized by Washington in reaction to the revolution.[21]

Enemies of the working class the world over gleefully predicted that the revolutionary government of Cuba would suffer a fate similar to the regimes of Eastern Europe and the USSR. But they failed to understand—as they had failed

---

20. Fidel Castro, speech marking twentieth anniversary of the death of Guevara, in *Socialism and Man in Cuba,* p. 50.

21. The events described in this section of Waters's presentation—the rectification process of the latter 1980s, and the special period that has marked the 1990s—are discussed in substantial detail in several issues of the Marxist magazine *New International.* See "Cuba's Rectification Process: Two Speeches by Fidel Castro" in issue no. 6 (1987); "The Politics of Economics: Che Guevara and Marxist Continuity" by Steve Clark and Jack Barnes in issue no. 8; and "Defending Cuba, Defending Cuba's Socialist Revolution" by Mary-Alice Waters in issue no. 10 (1994).

so many times before—that the proletarian internationalist course Che's name was associated with in Cuba and around the world was not his alone, but was indeed the trajectory of Cuba's communist leadership, deeply rooted among the big majority of Cuba's working people. This was not a variant of the course followed for decades in the Soviet Union and Eastern Europe, but its antipode. In the closing decade of the twentieth century, the Cuban people had once more set an example of historic import.

No other government in the world could have survived the test of popular support that Cuba's revolutionary leadership has faced in the 1990s, a support won in the course of many previous battles. Without an unblemished history of internationalism, without the broad political impact of hundreds of thousands of Cubans volunteering and taking part in missions abroad to aid and defend Grenada, Nicaragua, Ethiopia, and Angola, without a new generation of Cuban youth having learned in their own flesh and blood that "whoever is incapable of fighting for others will never be capable of fighting for himself,"[22] the future of the Cuban revolution would have been different.

Without the Cuban working class having previously begun to retake ground that had been lost to the economic planning technocrats, and the "communist[s] playing at capitalism,"[23] as Fidel called them, the Cuban revolution

---

22. Fidel Castro, speech at the December 5, 1988, Armed Forces Day celebration, in *In Defense of Socialism: Four Speeches on the 30th Anniversary of the Cuban Revolution* (New York: Pathfinder, 1989), p. 56 [2022 printing].

23. Fidel Castro, "Important Problems for the Whole of Revolutionary Thought," December 2, 1986, in *New International* no. 6, (1987), p. 361 [2023 printing]. Also found in *Granma Weekly Review,* December 14, 1986.

would have been in mortal danger as the crisis of the special period opened in 1990–91.

Without the tens of thousands of apartments, day-care centers, and doctor's offices built by the volunteer labor of the minibrigades, without the contingents that had taken the first steps toward beginning to transform the organization of labor in basic industry, the workers parliaments and efficiency assemblies that helped strengthen working-class resistance might not have been born. The capacity to organize a disciplined retreat—while holding the line at not one step further than necessary to assure the survival of proletarian power, of the revolutionary government—might not have been present.

Without the proletarian dignity regained by having previously charted a course to begin to deal with the worst abuses of power and privilege—as the Ochoa, de la Guardia, and Abrantes cases of 1989 exemplified[24]—the reserve of proletarian confidence and audacity necessary to once more say *"Sí se puede"* might not have been there.

• The special period through which Cuba is living today, whatever the factors that precipitated it, is not some unique

---

24. In July 1989 Arnaldo Ochoa, Antonio de la Guardia, and two other high-ranking officers of the Revolutionary Armed Forces and the Ministry of the Interior were sentenced to death for drug trafficking, abuse of office, and hostile acts against a foreign state (the Angolan government). One month later José Abrantes Fernández, Cuba's minister of the interior and, like Ochoa, a member of the Central Committee of the Communist Party, was sentenced to twenty years in prison on charges of abuse of authority, negligence in carrying out his duties, and improper use of government funds and resources. For a discussion of the position of the leadership of the Communist Party of Cuba on these events and their political significance as part of the rectification process in Cuba, see "Che's Proletarian Legacy and Cuba's Rectification Process" by Mary-Alice Waters in *New International* no. 8 (1991).

Cuban condition. It is a specific component of a reality imposed on working people the world over by the international capitalist market and an intensifying world depression.

World capitalism's 'special period'
A special period is what capitalism has in store for all of us. We need look no further than Mexico, Bosnia, or Malaysia if proof is needed. They are the first among others to come as the new century dawns. Under these conditions, Cuba's example and political weight in the world class struggle is growing once more. Cuba is showing how to fight for dignity, sovereignty, and independence, and why only a socialist course makes it possible for working people to hold their own against capital—anywhere in the world. There is no other way, as the Communist Manifesto describes, because "the need of a constantly expanding market for its products chases the bourgeoisie over the whole surface of the globe. It must nestle everywhere, settle everywhere, establish connections everywhere. . . . It compels all nations, on pain of extinction, to adopt the bourgeois mode of production; it compels them to introduce what it calls civilization into their midst, i.e., to become bourgeois themselves. In one word, it creates a world after its own image."[25]

But that is the world to which Cuban working people have said no, we will never go back. We will chart a different course, a course forward for humanity, a socialist course.

- Imperialism's growing world disorder and the "special periods" it has in store for us all are not something to

---

25. Marx and Engels, *The Communist Manifesto* (New York: Pathfinder, 1970, 1987, 2008), pp. 35–36 [2021 printing]. Also in Marx and Engels, *Collected Works,* vol. 6, pp. 487–88.

moan and cry about, as stunned liberals or aging radicals do. That would not be worthy of Che, whose true legacy many such individuals seek to redefine and wear as camouflage, nor of the Cuban revolution, whose lessons and example they often misremember or distort. In the words of the Second Declaration of Havana, "it is not for revolutionists to sit in the doorways of their houses waiting for the corpse of imperialism to pass by. The role of Job does not suit a revolutionist."[26]

Cuba is showing how to fight and why only a socialist course makes it possible for working people to hold their own against capital.

The world working class still faces what the Cuban people confronted in "the brilliant but sad days of the Caribbean crisis" of October 1962—the same "dangers and principles," the same possibility that one day a wounded imperialist beast, in a desperate attempt to save itself, will unleash its weapons of nuclear destruction, regardless of the consequences. In those "magnificent days," as Che called them[27]—recalling the courage, clarity, and calmness of the toilers and communist leadership in Cuba— one thing above all stayed Washington's hand. And it was neither Moscow, nor the missiles. It was the inability of imperialism to find cracks or divisions within the

---

26. *The First and Second Declarations of Havana,* pp. 74–75.

27. "Farewell letter to Fidel," in *Che Guevara Speaks,* p. 186.

command structure of the Revolutionary Armed Forces of Cuba and the sober estimate presented to the Kennedy administration by the U.S. armed forces chiefs of staff—stunned by the mobilization in a matter of days of 270,000 Cubans in arms—that U.S. forces would suffer an estimated 18,000 casualties in the first ten days of an attempted invasion of Cuba. That's more casualties than U.S. forces were to face in the first five years of Kennedy and Johnson's intervention in Vietnam—from 1961, when the first U.S. casualty was reported, to the middle of 1966.

That, and that alone, caused Washington to blink—and continues to do so today.

The interests of the world working class—and above all of the combined interests of the Cuban and U.S. working people—were equally served by the incomparable revolutionary determination of the Cuban people to resist, whatever the price, as Che put it in his Message to the Tricontinental, "compelling the U.S. imperialists to make a decision."

As we move into the twenty-first century, the world capitalist rulers find their options more and more restricted. The maintenance of their social order depends increasingly on balloons of debt forced upon others and inflated and unstable paper values, both inside and outside the imperialist centers. The resulting volatility brings growing insecurity into the lives of hundred of millions, deepening social inequality and accelerating political polarization. Once again we are witnessing how the logic of their system of domination—the imperialist reality—pushes them toward fascism and war.

To get there, however, the exploiters will have to face us first and try to defeat us. And, as the Cuban workers and farmers have shown the world for almost forty years, the outcome will be decided in struggle. Together with Fidel, in the spirit of Che and the Cuban revolution, we also say "Socialism or death!" That remains the only course of conduct that can win.

CUBA'S SOCIALIST REVOLUTION

New!
Revolution and the Road to Peace in Colombia
The Example of the Cuban Revolution
FIDEL CASTRO

"No crime can be committed in the name of revolution," Fidel Castro declares, drawing from the example set by working people of Cuba as they took state power out of the hands of its capitalist rulers. In 2008, as part of efforts to end six decades of armed conflict in Colombia, he shared the exemplary record of Cuba's revolutionary struggle with the Revolutionary Armed Forces of Colombia (FARC) and the world. $10. Also in Spanish.

Che Guevara on Economics and Politics in the Transition to Socialism
CARLOS TABLADA

It's essential for working people to win state power, said Ernesto Che Guevara. "Then there's the second stage, maybe more difficult than the first"—the transition from dog-eat-dog capitalism to socialism. Includes Fidel Castro's 1987 speech "Che's Ideas Are Absolutely Relevant Today." New edition with substantially expanded selections from Guevara's writings. $17. Also in Spanish.

To Speak the Truth
Why Washington's 'Cold War' Against Cuba Doesn't End
FIDEL CASTRO, CHE GUEVARA

In historic speeches before the United Nations and UN bodies, Guevara and Castro address the peoples of the world, explaining why the US government so fears the example set by the socialist revolution in Cuba. $15

BUILDING A PROLETARIAN PARTY

Malcolm X, Black Liberation, and the Road to Workers Power
JACK BARNES

"The conquest of state power by a class-conscious vanguard of the working class is the mightiest weapon possible in the fight against Black oppression, the subjugation of women, Jew-hatred, and every form of human degradation inherited from class society." $20. Also in Spanish, French, Farsi, Arabic, Greek.

The Turn to Industry
Forging a Proletarian Party
JACK BARNES

A book about the working-class program, composition, and course of the only kind of party in the imperialist epoch worthy of the name "revolutionary." A party that can recognize the most revolutionary fact of this epoch—the worth of working people, and our capacity to change society when we organize and act to win power from the capitalist class. $15. Also in Spanish, French, Farsi, Greek.

The Communist Manifesto
KARL MARX AND FREDERICK ENGELS

Communism, say the founding leaders of the revolutionary workers movement, is not a set of ideas or preconceived "principles" but workers' line of march to power. It springs from a "movement going on under our very eyes." $5. Also in Spanish, French, Farsi, Arabic.

PATHFINDERPRESS.COM

ALSO FROM PATHFINDER

The Low Point of Labor Resistance Is Behind Us
The Socialist Workers Party Looks Forward
JACK BARNES, MARY-ALICE WATERS STEVE CLARK

The global order imposed by Washington is shattering. A long retreat by the working class and unions has come to an end. The bosses and their government are stepping up attacks on our wages, conditions, and constitutional rights. This book highlights opportunities for building a mass proletarian party able to lead the struggle to end capitalist rule, opening a socialist future for humanity. $10. Also in Spanish, French, Greek.

Cuba and the Coming American Revolution
JACK BARNES

This is a book about the example set by the Cuban people that socialist revolution is not only necessary—it can be made. A book about the struggles of workers and other exploited producers in the imperialist heartland, and the youth attracted to them. About the class struggle in the US, where the revolutionary capacities of working people are as utterly discounted by the ruling powers as were those of the Cuban toilers. $10. Also in Spanish, French, Farsi.

Labor, Nature, and the Evolution of Humanity
The Long View of History
FREDERICK ENGELS, KARL MARX
GEORGE NOVACK, MARY-ALICE WATERS

Without understanding that social labor, transforming nature, has driven humanity's evolution for millions of years, working people are unable to see beyond the capitalist epoch of class exploitation that warps all human relations, ideas, and values. $12. Also in Spanish and French.

New Expanded Edition!
Cosmetics, Fashion, and the Exploitation of Women
MARY-ALICE WATERS
JOSEPH HANSEN, EVELYN REED

"Norms of beauty and fashion are inseparable from the class struggle." That's the title of the opening chapter of this timely new edition of a lively 1950s debate in the *Militant*, a socialist newsweekly. How cosmetics and fashion monopolies rake in profits from social insecurities of women and adolescents. Why women's integration into the workforce and unions is a major advance in the fight for emancipation. A Marxist classic on the origins of women's oppression and the working-class road forward. $15. Also in Spanish, French, Farsi, Greek.

The Fight Against Jew-Hatred and Pogroms in the Imperialist Epoch
Stakes for the International Working Class

V.I. LENIN, LEON TROTSKY
FARRELL DOBBS, JAMES P. CANNON
JACK BARNES, DAVE PRINCE

Jew-hatred and pogroms—such as Hamas carried out on October 7, 2023—are part of the social convulsions and wars of the imperialist epoch. The authors explain why fighting Jew-hatred is decisive to the working class and oppressed nations of the world—and *what is to be done* to end it. $10. Also in Spanish, French, Greek.

Imperialism's March Toward Fascism and War
JACK BARNES

"There will be new Hitlers, new Mussolinis. That is inevitable. What is not inevitable is that they will triumph. The working-class vanguard will organize our class to fight back against the devastating toll we are made to pay for the capitalist crisis. The future of humanity will be decided in the contest between these contending class forces." In *New International* no. 10. $14. Also in Spanish, French, Farsi, Greek.

PATHFINDERPRESS.COM

PATHFINDER AROUND THE WORLD

UNITED STATES
(and Caribbean, Latin America, and East Asia)

*Pathfinder Books, 306 W. 37th St., 13th Floor
New York, NY 10018*

CANADA

*Pathfinder Books, 7107 St. Denis, Suite 204
Montreal, QC H2S 2S5*

UNITED KINGDOM
(and Europe, Africa, Middle East, and South Asia)

*Pathfinder Books, 5 Norman Rd.
Seven Sisters, London N15 4ND*

AUSTRALIA
(and New Zealand, Southeast Asia, and the Pacific)

*Pathfinder Books, Suite 2, First floor, 275 George St.
Liverpool, Sydney, NSW 2170
Postal address: P.O. Box 73, Campsie, NSW 2194*

BUILD YOUR LIBRARY!
JOIN THE PATHFINDER READERS CLUB

**$10 / YEAR
25% DISCOUNT ON ALL PATHFINDER TITLES
30% OFF BOOKS OF THE MONTH**

Valid at pathfinderpress.com and local Pathfinder book centers

Go to: pathfinderpress.com/
products/pathfinder-readers-club

Pathfinder
pathfinderpress.com